D1375602

EU GDPR

A Pocket Guide

ALAN CALDER

IT Governance Publishing

Every possible effort has been made to ensure that the information contained in this book is accurate at the time of going to press, and the publisher and the author cannot accept responsibility for any errors or omissions, however caused. Any opinions expressed in this book are those of the author, not the publisher. Websites identified are for reference only, not endorsement, and any website visits are at the reader's own risk. No responsibility for loss or damage occasioned to any person acting, or refraining from action, as a result of the material in this publication can be accepted by the publisher or the author.

Apart from any fair dealing for the purposes of research or private study, or criticism or review, as permitted under the Copyright, Designs and Patents Act 1988, this publication may only be reproduced, stored or transmitted, in any form, or by any means, with the prior permission in writing of the publisher or, in the case of reprographic reproduction, in accordance with the terms of licences issued by the Copyright Licensing Agency. Enquiries concerning reproduction outside those terms should be sent to the publisher at the following address:

IT Governance Publishing
IT Governance Limited
Unit 3, Clive Court
Bartholomew's Walk
Cambridgeshire Business Park
Ely, Cambridgeshire
CB7 4EA
United Kingdom

www.itgovernance.co.uk

The author has asserted the rights of the author under the Copyright, Designs and Patents Act, 1988, to be identified as the author of this work.

First published in the United Kingdom in 2016
by IT Governance Publishing.

ISBN 978-1-84928-831-6

ABOUT THE AUTHOR

Alan Calder is the founder and executive chairman of IT Governance Ltd (*www.itgovernance.co.uk*), an information, advice and consultancy firm that helps company boards tackle IT governance, risk management, compliance and information security issues. He has many years of senior management experience in the private and public sectors.

The company operates websites around the world that distribute a range of books, tools and other publications on IT governance, risk management, compliance and information security.

CONTENTS

Contents

INTRODUCTION

Few companies are in favour of further regulation, but it's generally recognised that it has a role to play in keeping industries honest and protecting the populace at large. There's also a lot of opposition to particularly strong regulation, so more heavy-handed laws are often developed incrementally, which conveniently reduces the outcry at any given stage. It's quite rare for a particularly strong regulation to come about all at once: the European Union's General Data Protection Regulation (GDPR) is one such beast, however.

It's not that the Regulation is unnecessary, nor that any individual requirement is particularly egregious; rather, much of the challenge is that it has come along all at once and could potentially affect nearly every organisation in the world. The Regulation is so widely applicable, in fact, that there are likely to be legal arguments and discussions over the coming decade to determine the true extent of its powers[1]. Regardless of how well it holds up, every business in Europe – and a substantial number in other jurisdictions – should be prepared to deal with the repercussions.

And those repercussions are not to be sneezed at: organisations found to be in breach of the Regulation can be fined up to €20 million, or four percent of global annual turnover – whichever is the greatest. Needless to say, there are few companies that would be willing to take a hit of that magnitude when compliance can be achieved much, much more cheaply.

So, on the face of it, the Regulation is quite a terrifying prospect: it will certainly force every organisation in the EU to increase its compliance spending, it will have a significant

---

[1] There's more on this in Chapter 3 of this guide (The Regulation).

impact on how those organisations gather data and how it's organised, and it's backed by the threat of substantial fines. Equally, however, the Regulation itself notes that it aims to tread that line between protecting the rights of the individual and removing barriers to the "free movement of personal data within the internal market". That is, while the Regulation places limits and restrictions on the use and storage of personal data (sometimes called 'personally identifiable information', or PII), it does so in the interests of both keeping the EU at the forefront of the modern information economy, while ensuring an 'equal playing field' among the member countries of the EU.

Those organisations that appreciate this distinction, and act quickly to resolve issues and to ensure compliance with the Regulation, will be the ones that thrive in the evolving regulatory environment. There's also room for significant process improvements for organisations that already operate internationally within the EU: by standardising the requirements for data protection, organisations can also streamline their processes, which may realise significant efficiency improvements while minimising the risk of compliance issues.

This pocket guide aims to help you thrive under these new conditions by providing you with an understanding of the Regulation, the broader principles of data protection, and what the Regulation means for businesses in Europe and beyond.

There are key terms throughout this book that need to be properly understood to really get to grips with the new Regulation, which are defined in Chapter 2 – Terms and definitions.

CHAPTER 1: A BRIEF HISTORY OF DATA PROTECTION

The common conception of data protection is a very modern notion. We think of digitally stored databases and records, and we understand the importance of protecting them. It's obvious: digital records have no physical weight, and can be mislaid or stolen without removing the original, and it's easy to comprehend that such a loss could represent an enormous amount of information. This isn't the way it's always been, though, and even today information in other formats needs to be protected.

Possibly the earliest forms of data and privacy protection come from the professions rather than legislation itself. Lawyer-client confidentiality (or legal professional privilege, as it's called in the UK), for instance, is believed to have begun as a sort of contract between a lawyer and their client many decades (and possibly centuries) before it entered into law itself. It was introduced as a way of ensuring that a lawyer could adequately represent their clients' interests without the client fearing legal repercussions.

Equally, the keeping of medical records and a doctor's confidentiality were established decades ago, and, while a court could force those records to be handed over, the medical profession otherwise kept them relatively safe. Once again, this was something that the profession handled long before the law moved to codify the practice.

Under these practices, specific silos of personal information were protected according to the interests of the business: if a profession could see the business value in protecting information, it was protected. This has had to change, however, as record keeping shifted from paper to electronics, and as the methods for manipulating even small elements of personal information have become more powerful, which puts all this information at risk because it now has a distinct value. Political campaigns, as a *reasonably* ethical example, have used increasing volumes of data to better target key demographics, define policy, manage candidates' image and so on. On the other end of the scale, identity theft has become a significant problem that has only become a greater threat with the greater volume of information that is available.

With regard to the situation in Europe, one of the first legal protections for personal information was codified in Article 8 of the European Convention on Human Rights (ECHR) in 1953. This wasn't in the form that we might expect to see privacy legislation today, but it provides the foundation for modern European privacy laws. Article 8 reads:

1. Everyone has the right to respect for his private and family life, his home and his correspondence.

2. There shall be no interference by a public authority with the exercise of this right except such as is in accordance with the law and is necessary in a democratic society in the interests of national security, public safety or the economic well-being of the country, for the prevention of disorder or crime, for the protection of health or morals, or for the protection of the rights and freedoms of others.

There is some criticism that this is an unnecessarily open-ended provision, as unscrupulous people could interpret it in order to restrict the rights of the people (through the application of laws to circumvent some of the protections, which are permitted), to place undue regulatory burden on third parties (through the application of laws that use equally broad language) and to limit the power of the state to pursue justice (because the European Court of Human Rights will almost always find against any laws that could violate the right to privacy[2]). Obviously, these are conflicting opinions, so it has remained generally balanced in the interests of all parties.

Regardless of its interpretation, the ECHR's legacy with regard to the right to privacy has carried down through the decades into our modern legal landscape.

In 1981, the Council of Europe established standards to ensure the free flow of information throughout EU member countries without infringing personal privacy. The convention that enacted these standards – the Convention for the Protection of Individuals with regard to Automatic Processing of Personal Data – was developed in response to the burgeoning use of computers to store and process personal data. The minimum standards it set then became the basis of the first round of privacy laws across Europe.

In 1984, the UK introduced its first Data Protection Act, which introduced basic rules governing the storage and processing of personal data in the UK. These rules accommodated the minimum standards specified in the EU's 1981 convention, and thus weren't particularly rigorous – in 1984, of course, requirements for the protection of personal data were considerably less urgent than today.

As we know, however, the power and availability of computers exploded during the 80s and 90s, and by 1995 more than a million people in the UK were regularly using the Internet. Furthermore, over the years since the Convention was applied, EU Member States' data protection laws had diverged, which began impeding the flow of data through the European Union – and thus impeding business. It was quite clear that existing data protection regimes across Europe were inadequate to support

---

[2] Especially if those laws seem to contravene or impinge on other articles in the ECHR, such as Article 10 – the right to freedom of expression and information.

Articles 8 and 10 of the ECHR, and so the Data Protection Directive (DPD) was enacted in 1995.

The DPD required EU member states to respond by developing laws of their own to meet new, more rigorous minimum standards, and taking into account the significantly more powerful, readily available and affordable computers and electronic devices. It was functionally a 'reset' for data protection, obliging all member states to align with it and thereby improve protections for personal data, while simultaneously reducing the burdens impeding the free flow of data through the Union.

The DPD also established rules for the transport of personal data outside of the EU. This was most famously reflected in the US-EU Safe Harbor framework, which asserted that US data protection laws were sufficient for the protection of personal data originating in the EU, as long as the recipient in the US observed a set of data protection principles. While this framework was found to be in breach of the DPD in 2015, it did support considerable business activity for 15 years.

The UK's Data Protection Act of 1998 was the British law that enacted the requirements of the DPD and was founded on eight principles. These principles clearly laid out the general aims of the Act, which made it reasonably simple to determine whether an organisation was meeting its obligations. There was some complexity in the broader Act, however, and repeated amendments and updates meant that it continued to grow and become more unwieldy as time went on.

In Germany, meanwhile, data protection was primarily regulated through the Federal Data Protection Act (Bundesdatenschutzgesetz, BDSG), supported by a number of sector-specific regulations at varying levels of federal and state government. Because it also sought to meet the requirements of the DPD, this law was broadly comparable to the UK's DPA, but with considerable differences in the detail.

France's Data Protection Act (Loi informatique et libertés, LIL) dates back to 1978, predating many other national data protection laws and covering the lifespan of both the EU convention and the DPD. Rather than developing new laws in response to those pressures from the European Union, the French legislature instead opted to amend its existing law. Despite this, the LIL we see today is surprisingly concise.

Across the EU, other, similar legislation was enacted, but through a combination of time and varying national interests, no two national laws were sufficiently similar for an organisation to simultaneously be compliant in its home country and across all the other EU member states. That is, the free flow of information was effectively inhibited because the different regulatory environments clashed on matters of detail, requiring businesses and governments alike to arrange processes specific to an increasing array of scenarios. It is this, in conjunction with the steady march of technological progress, that created the environment into which the General Data Protection Regulation was born.

That the solution is a regulation rather than a directive (as the DPD was) is worthy of discussion. Within EU law, a directive sets out minimum conditions or requirements but does not pass any specific measures in itself. That is, an individual or organisation is not required to be in compliance with a directive. Rather, each Member State is obliged to pass its own laws in order to meet the minimum requirements of the directive, and this is what organisations and individuals have to comply with.

A regulation, meanwhile, is functionally a law and enters into force across the Union simultaneously. No Member State needs to pass additional laws in order to bring it into force, and it is not dependent on the interpretation of the local government, courts or authorities. Because of the legal weight of a regulation, they typically take much longer to pass through the legislative process, but they also ensure greater consistency across the Union.

The GDPR had a particularly long and arduous journey on its way to approval by the European Parliament and Council, and it was not without controversy. Over the several years it spent in committee stages, being written and rewritten – it had thousands of amendments proposed, pushing for more or less data privacy – the more contentious points were gradually eradicated, however.

CHAPTER 2: TERMS AND DEFINITIONS

Before getting into the meat of the Regulation and how you can comply with it, it's useful to have a set of definitions for common and useful terms. Where the Regulation provides a definition, this is included, and any additional commentary has been added where useful.

Binding corporate rules

> personal data protection policies which are adhered to by a controller or processor established on the territory of a Member State for transfers or a set of transfers of personal data to a controller or processor in one or more third countries within a group of undertakings, or group of enterprises engaged in a joint economic activity;[3]

Binding corporate rules were originally devised by the Article 29 Working Party (a group within the EU that develops and promotes good practices for data protection) in order to allow large organisations, or groups of organisations, to securely transfer data internationally while reducing bureaucratic interference. The GDPR establishes conditions for individual Member States to establish their own binding corporate rules to streamline international transfers.

Biometric data

> personal data resulting from specific technical processing relating to the physical, physiological or behavioural characteristics of a natural person, which allow or confirm

---

[3] EU GDPR, Article 4 (20).

the unique identification of that natural person, such as facial images or dactyloscopic data;[4]

Biometric data is increasingly used as a method of authentication, and often in conjunction with other data that should be protected (such as passwords, and, by extension, whatever information can be accessed as a result of gaining access to this). Member States are permitted to introduce further restrictions or conditions regarding the processing of biometric data.

Consent

any freely given, specific, informed and unambiguous indication of the data subject's wishes by which he or she, by a statement or by a clear affirmative action, signifies agreement to the processing of personal data relating to him or her;[5]

Consent is an incredibly important concept in the GDPR, and is covered extensively later in this book.

Cross-border processing

(a) processing of personal data which takes place in the context of the activities of establishments in more than one Member State of a controller or processor in the Union where the controller or processor is established in more than one Member State; or

(b) processing of personal data which takes place in the context of the activities of a single establishment of a controller or processor in the Union but which

---

[4] EU GDPR, Article 4 (14).
[5] EU GDPR, Article 4 (11).

> substantially affects or is likely to substantially affect data subjects in more than one Member State.[6]

This refers to data transfers within the European Union; where this occurs, the Regulation has stipulations as to which supervisory authority is to be involved.

Data concerning health

> personal data related to the physical or mental health of a natural person, including the provision of health care services, which reveal information about his or her health status;[7]

Health data is awarded particular protections under the Regulation in order to protect the vulnerable. While all personal data is to be protected, some forms – such as health data – have additional restrictions as to how and when it can be processed, and the level of consent required to authorise the processing. Member States are permitted to introduce further restrictions or conditions regarding the processing of data concerning health.

Data controllers

> the natural or legal person, public authority, agency or other body which, alone or jointly with others, determines the purposes and means of the processing of personal data; where the purposes and means of such processing are determined by Union or Member State law, the controller or the specific criteria for its nomination may be provided for by Union or Member State law;[8]

These will usually be the 'public-facing' entities that data subjects supply their information to. For instance, a hospital

---

[6] EU GDPR, Article 4 (23).
[7] EU GDPR, Article 4 (15).
[8] EU GDPR, Article 4 (7).

might have an online form for entering health information; even if the online form is provided by a third party, the hospital (which will determine what the data is processed for) will be the data controller.

Data processors

> a natural or legal person, public authority, agency or other body which processes personal data on behalf of the controller;[9]

In many cases, the data controller and the data processor will be the same entity. In the example above, the organisation that provides the online form will be a data processor because the act of collecting data is included within the definition of 'processing'.[10] A single data controller may have several data processors.

Data subject

The Regulation defines a data subject as "an identified or identifiable natural person".[11] There is no restriction on their nationality or place of residence, however, so a data subject can be from anywhere in the world – the Regulation does not distinguish. Equally, however, a data subject has to be a *person*; a corporation or other entity cannot be a data subject, and information on those subjects has no protection under the Regulation.

Filing system

> any structured set of personal data which are accessible according to specific criteria, whether centralised,

---

[9] EU GDPR, Article 4 (8).
[10] EU GDPR, Article 4 (2).
[11] EU GDPR, Article 4 (1).

decentralised or dispersed on a functional or geographical basis;[12]

This is used as a generic term to cover all methods by which personal data can be collected, stored, transmitted and processed.

Genetic data

> personal data relating to the inherited or acquired genetic characteristics of a natural person which give unique information about the physiology or the health of that natural person and which result, in particular, from an analysis of a biological sample from the natural person in question;[13]

With the increasing interest in genetics and genetic engineering, and public concerns over the legal status of genetic data, the Regulation includes genetic data as part of personal data, thereby providing it with protections at least equal to other personal data. Member States are permitted to introduce further restrictions or conditions regarding the processing of genetic data.

Main establishment

> (a) as regards a controller with establishments in more than one Member State, the place of its central administration in the Union, unless the decisions on the purposes and means of the processing of personal data are taken in another establishment of the controller in the Union and the latter establishment has the power to have such decisions implemented, in which case the establishment

---

[12] EU GDPR, Article 4 (6).
[13] EU GDPR, Article 4 (13).

having taken such decisions is to be considered to be the main establishment;

(b) as regards a processor with establishments in more than one Member State, the place of its central administration in the Union, or, if the processor has no central administration in the Union, the establishment of the processor in the Union where the main processing activities in the context of the activities of an establishment of the processor take place to the extent that the processor is subject to specific obligations under this Regulation;[14]

Determining the 'main establishment' for organisations with a presence in multiple Member States will be important, as this defines which supervisory authority is to be involved, and may have some impact on various restrictions and conditions on processing certain types of personal data (such as biometric, genetic and health data).

Personal data

'personal data' means any information relating to an identified or identifiable natural person ('data subject'); an identifiable natural person is one who can be identified, directly or indirectly, in particular by reference to an identifier such as a name, an identification number, location data, an online identifier or to one or more factors specific to the physical, physiological, genetic, mental, economic, cultural or social identity of that natural person;[15]

Of specific note here is that the set of characteristics above is not exhaustive: *any* information that could be used to identify the data subject is personal data, and this information can be in

---

[14] EU GDPR, Article 4 (16).
[15] EU GDPR, Article 4 (1).

any format. This can encompass photographs, correspondence, physical media and so on.

Personal data breach

> a breach of security leading to the accidental or unlawful destruction, loss, alteration, unauthorised disclosure of, or access to, personal data transmitted, stored or otherwise processed;[16]

The majority of data breaches that the Regulation is concerned with are personal data breaches. More general data breaches will be of concern if the data that is lost could lead to a personal data breach.

Processing

> 'processing' means any operation or set of operations which is performed on personal data or on sets of personal data, whether or not by automated means, such as collection, recording, organisation, structuring, storage, adaptation or alteration, retrieval, consultation, use, disclosure by transmission, dissemination or otherwise making available, alignment or combination, restriction, erasure or destruction;[17]

This is an extremely broad definition but, again, it is not exhaustive. Functionally, processing may include any interaction you have with personal data, in whatever form it takes. Establishing the full range of processing that you are responsible for will be a significant part of complying with the Regulation.

---

[16] EU GDPR, Article 4 (12).
[17] EU GDPR, Article 4 (2).

Profiling

> any form of automated processing of personal data consisting of the use of personal data to evaluate certain personal aspects relating to a natural person, in particular to analyse or predict aspects concerning that natural person's performance at work, economic situation, health, personal preferences, interests, reliability, behaviour, location or movements;[18]

Data subjects must always be informed if any profiling processes will be performed on their personal data before they consent.

Pseudonymisation

> the processing of personal data in such a manner that the personal data can no longer be attributed to a specific data subject without the use of additional information, provided that such additional information is kept separately and is subject to technical and organisational measures to ensure that the personal data are not attributed to an identified or identifiable natural person;[19]

While the Regulation generally considers pseudonymisation to be a positive thing, it does also specify that pseudonymised data that can be "attributed to a natural person by the use of additional information should be considered to be information on an identifiable natural person".[20] As such, any organisation that uses pseudonymisation to protect personal data should ensure that it is not possible to identify the original data subject if additional information is made available. As noted in the definition, this should include measures to completely separate pseudonymised data from all other personal data.

---

[18] EU GDPR, Article 4 (4).
[19] EU GDPR, Article 4 (5).
[20] EU GDPR, Recital 26.

Representative

> a natural or legal person established in the Union who, designated by the controller or processor in writing pursuant to Article 27, represents the controller or processor with regard to their respective obligations under this Regulation;[21]

Organisations (both data controllers and data processors) that are not established in the EU but wish to conduct processing in line with Article 27, must appoint a representative that is established in the EU. This ensures that all significant personal data collection and processing has a presence within the Union and ready contact with authorities.

Supervisory authority

> 'supervisory authority' means an independent public authority which is established by a Member State pursuant to Article 51;[22]

In most cases, the supervisory authority will be the authority currently responsible for data protection measures. In the UK, for instance, it will most likely be the Information Commissioner's Office.

---

[21] EU GDPR, Article 4 (17)
[22] EU GDPR, Article 4 (21).

CHAPTER 3: THE REGULATION

The GDPR was adopted by the EU Council and Parliament in April 2016, and will take effect in every EU member state in May 2018. As of the time of writing this book, there is a bit less than two years in which organisations can prepare to meet its requirements. The GDPR is a long document, though, and sets out requirements for organisations and for Member States, and makes provision for the creation of an EU Data Protection Board. This chapter aims to provide a quick overview of the key points that you need to be aware of in order to prepare for compliance.

The full text of the GDPR can be found on the EUR-Lex database (*http://eur-lex.europa.eu/*) in every language of the European Union.[23] For organisations in the UK, the Information Commissioner's Office has established a microsite dealing specifically with data protection reform, including the GDPR, and this will operate as a centralised source of information on how the Regulation is to be applied in the UK. This is available at *https://ico.org.uk/for-organisations/data-protection-reform/*.

While you will undoubtedly need to engage with your professional advisers in order to ensure that your legal documentation is all amended to comply with the GDPR, this Pocket Guide will give you a far less expensive overview of the requirements and your route to compliance.

---

[23] The full text of the Regulation can be found in English at *http://eur-lex.europa.eu/legal-content/EN/TXT/PDF/?uri=CELEX:52012PC0011&rid=2* or on the European Council's open database at *http://data.consilium.europa.eu/doc/document/ST-5419-2016-INIT/en/pdf*.

Failure to meet the requirements of the Regulation could also turn out to be an expensive error. The Regulation specifies that administrative fines are to follow "appropriate procedural safeguards in accordance with Union and Member State law, including effective judicial remedy and due process",[24] so organisations will not be fined summarily. The Regulation also states that the fines are intended to be "effective, proportionate and dissuasive",[25] so you can assume that the intent is that they won't be needed: the threat of such fines should, ideally, ensure that all data controllers and data processors will comply.

Infringements of some Articles carry the maximum administrative penalty (as noted, up to four percent of annual global turnover or €20 million, whichever is greater). Infringements of the requirements in relation to international transfers are also subject to this higher penalty.

The higher penalties apply to the following Articles:

- 5 – Principles relating to processing of personal data
- 6 – Lawfulness of processing
- 7 – Conditions for consent
- 9 – Processing of special categories of personal data
- 12 – Transparent information, communication and modalities for the exercise of the rights of the data subject
- 13 – Information to be provided where personal data are collected from the data subject
- 14 – Information to be provided where personal data have not been obtained from the data subject

---

[24] EU GDPR, Article 83 (8).
[25] EU GDPR, Article 83 (1).

- 15 – Right of access by the data subject

- 16 – Right to rectification

- 17 – Right to erasure ('right to be forgotten')

- 18 – Right to restriction of processing

- 19 – Notification obligation regarding rectification or erasure of personal data or restriction of processing

- 20 – Right to data portability

- 21 – Right to object

- 22 – Automated individual decision-making, including profiling

There is also a lower rate of penalty for infringing other Articles of the Regulation, which is calculated at up to two percent of global annual turnover or €10 million – again, whichever is higher. This will apply to the following Articles:

- 8 – Conditions applicable to child's consent in relation to information society services

- 11 – Processing which does not require identification

- 25 – Data protection by design and by default

- 26 – Joint controllers

- 27 – Representatives of controllers or processors not established in the Union

- 28 – Processor

- 29 – Processing under the authority of the controller or processor

- 30 – Records of processing activities

- 31 – Cooperation with the supervisory authority

- 32 – Security of processing

- 33 – Notification of personal data breach to the supervisory authority

- 34 – Communication of a personal data breach to the data subject

- 35 – Data protection impact assessment

- 36 – Prior consultation

- 37 – Designation of the data protection officer

- 38 – Position of the data protection officer

- 39 – Tasks of the data protection officer

- 42 – Certification

- 43 – Certification bodies

Principles

Article 5 of the GDPR outlines the six principles that should be applied to any collection or processing of personal data.

1. Personal data must be processed lawfully, fairly and transparently.

2. Personal data can only be collected for specified, explicit and legitimate purposes.

3. Personal data must be adequate, relevant and limited to what is necessary for processing.

4. Personal data must be accurate and kept up to date.

5. Personal data must be kept in a form such that the data subject can be identified only as long as is necessary for processing.

6. Personal data must be processed in a manner that ensures its security.

It's worth noting that the data controller is responsible for demonstrating this, and they must secure the same assurances from any external data processors with whom they contract.

These six principles are at the heart of the Regulation in much the same way that the eight principles of the UK's Data Protection Act are at the heart of that law. You should be clear on what each of them mean, however, especially as some terms are considerably broader than you might otherwise expect (such as 'processing' – a full definition is provided in the previous chapter).

Fundamentally, if you can demonstrate that you're meeting these requirements, it is likely that you're in a good position to meet your GDPR compliance requirements, but it's also extremely likely that there are some aspects of the Regulation that you simply haven't accounted for.

Applicability

The GDPR applies to organisations within the EU, and to any external organisations that are trading within the EU. This potentially includes organisations everywhere in the world, regardless of how difficult it may be to enforce the Regulation. This extensive reach is likely, however, to keep European organisations from working with companies and states that fail to meet the Regulation's requirements. This is because the Regulation asserts that both the data controller (likely to be within the EU) and the data processor are liable in the event of a data breach. With the impressively threatening fines hovering overhead like a sword of Damocles, there are few organisations that will be willing to risk working with an organisation outside the EU that cannot prove its ability to protect the personal data it is given.

The information that the Regulation aims to protect is that of "natural persons, whatever their nationality or place of residence". It should be noted that, unlike some commentary that has mistakenly claimed it applies only to EU citizens, it accounts for other residents of the European Union, including refugees, people on work and travel visas, those with residency, and so on, and could also be taken to apply to non-EU residents whose personal data is held and/or processed within the EU. On the face of it, EU organisations bound by the Regulation must protect personal data about *anyone* from *anywhere* in the world. Naturally, this is going to be difficult to enforce on organisations based outside the EU, but it is important to remember that the Regulation does not distinguish between data subjects on the basis of nationality or location.

The personal data that the Regulation refers to is now much broader than that which was protected under the DPD and the varying acts of legislation that supported it. The GDPR states that the personal data it is concerned with is:

> any information relating to an identified or identifiable natural person ('data subject'); an identifiable person is one who can be identified, directly or indirectly, in particular by reference to an identifier, such as a name, an identification number, location data, an online identifier or to one or more factors specific to the physical, physiological, genetic, mental, economic, cultural or social identity of that natural person;[26]

This extended list of characteristics means that a great deal of anonymised data may no longer be suitable for distribution or sharing in public. At the very least, organisations that distribute anonymised data will need to carefully assess whether the data can be linked – directly or indirectly – to the actual subject. This list of characteristics is also not exhaustive, so *any* information that could be used to identify the data subject should be subject to the same protections.

---

[26] EU GDPR, Article 4 (1).

Data subjects' rights

The GDPR considerably increases the rights of data subjects. Much has been made of this in the news – especially the 'right to be forgotten' – but the Regulation does attempt to balance those rights against the right to the free flow of information in order to support "the pursuit of economic activities". The expanded rights granted to data subjects can generally be characterised as giving them more control over their data and giving them a better understanding of what is being done with it.

From the organisation's point of view, this means that you will need to ensure that you are clear about what data you are collecting and what you will be using it for. This is likely to be a significant change for most organisations, but it will be critical because many of the restrictions on processing in the Regulation have caveats that apply if the data subject has explicitly consented. While you might not think that your particular data processing will need to invoke one of these caveats, the actual rules on what can be done without specific consent are surprisingly restrictive.

Should their rights be infringed, data subjects will be able to seek judicial remedies against controllers and processors, and will also have the right to seek compensation from controllers or processors for damages arising from breaches of the GDPR. Data subjects will also have the right under Article 77 to lodge a complaint with their relevant data protection authority (called a 'supervisory authority' in the Regulation – more on this later) if they believe the processing of their personal data infringes the GDPR. More generally, controllers will now be directly "liable for the damage caused by processing which infringes" the GDPR. As previously noted, this ensures that the controller has a vested interest in ensuring the security of any personal data that they pass to a processor, whether the processor is inside or outside the European Union.

Consent

In general, you have to have a data subject's consent to process their data. While there are specific circumstances in which consent is not strictly necessary, these generally revolve around legal requirements (such as in compliance with another law, or in order to protect the rights of a data subject), or where the data subject's consent is provided through a contract they have with a third party. Beyond these sorts of exemptions, you will need to ensure that you secure consent for processing any data subject's personal information.

Data controllers will have to ensure that they secure clear and unambiguous consent from the data subject before processing personal data. Critically, the controller is not permitted to count "Silence, pre-ticked boxes or inactivity"[27] as consent. Furthermore, processing cannot proceed unless the data subject has consented to every processing activity – if you wish to carry out six different actions with the subject's data, for instance, you need to ensure that the subject has consented to all of them.

This is quite a change from the requirements of the DPD, which permitted implicit and 'opt-out' consent under some circumstances. Children under 16 are also no longer able to consent to having their personal data processed, which could force some organisations to make significant changes to the way they operate, as obtaining consent from the "holder of parental responsibility" may be anywhere between difficult to impossible. Article 8 provides further information on this, but it does not describe specifically how to resolve the problem, nor how supervisory authorities might determine that you have met the requirements of the Regulation.

The Regulation notes that consent can be provided electronically using a tick-box (although, as noted above, the

---

[27] EU GDPR, Recital 32.

data subject will have to manually tick the box themselves), which is in line with the way many organisations already ensure appropriate consent for specific activities. However, because of the notorious unreliability of the user with regard to terms and conditions (and because, in the past, companies have found themselves in court over the use of fine print in such documents), the GDPR requires that the consent document be laid out in simple terms. In the words of the Regulation, "the request must be clear, concise and not unnecessarily disruptive to the use of the service for which it is provided".[28] This final point may be problematic, especially where you require consent for a variety of activities.

Documentation of consent is crucial, and this is one key area in which legal input from your professional advisers is essential.

Finally, consent can be withdrawn. Few organisations have a formal, efficient process in place for allowing data subjects to remove consent, however, and – much like securing consent in the first place – the Regulation requires the data controller to provide a method whereby it is "as easy to withdraw consent as to give it".[29] Web application developers will no doubt need to design and implement robust solutions to allow data subjects to withdraw their consent in accordance with this requirement.

Right to be forgotten

Data subjects have the right to have any data held about them erased under a number of circumstances, and this must also occur if they withdraw consent for all of the processing for which the data is held. This is functionally quite a broad right. Organisations will not have a particularly large range of options for refusing to erase personal data, so should look into

---

[28] EU GDPR, Recital 32.
[29] EU GDPR, Article 7 (3).

establishing a process to erase all such data as and when necessary.

While this might seem quite straightforward, the data controller must also take "reasonable steps" to erase any of the data subject's personal data that might be public, such as in news articles or databases. As anyone who understands the Internet knows, this is barely possible – the variety of archive databases assure that – but it is quite likely that the data protection authority in your country will still want to see that a concerted effort has been made, and that all appropriate technical and procedural measures to erase the data have been employed.

Data portability

Under Article 20 of the Regulation, data subjects can request a copy of any personal data held on them, and can also request that this information is transmitted to another data controller. The Regulation doesn't stipulate precisely how this information has to be presented or the format it has to be in, but it does require that it is in a "structured, commonly used and machine-readable format".

While this shouldn't present too much of a difficulty to most organisations, determining an appropriate format before you're asked to supply the information is a sensible step. Much like freedom of information requests, the key is to ensure that the process is inexpensive and efficient.

Some businesses will already have appropriate contact with other organisations to facilitate the transfer of data – banks in the UK, for instance – and these contacts could be leveraged to streamline this process.

Lawful processing

As noted earlier, controllers are accountable for ensuring that personal data is lawfully, fairly and transparently processed.

The lawfulness of processing is expanded in Article 6, which clarifies that this ensures that the data subject must have given consent (thus including all of the requirements of consent noted earlier), or that the processing is necessary for certain tasks, the majority of which require consideration of the data subject's interests.

It is worth noting that processing is permissible if it is "necessary for the purposes of the legitimate interests pursued by the controller or by a third party, except where such interests are overridden by the interests or fundamental rights and freedoms of the data subject which require protection of personal data, in particular where the data subject is a child".[30] While this caveat essentially makes lawful any reasonable processing in line with your organisation's interests, you must ensure that it does not otherwise threaten the interests, rights or freedoms of the data subject, is not in contravention of some other law or regulation (at the local, national or Union level), and is "necessary for the performance of a task carried out in the public interest or in the exercise of official authority vested in the controller".[31] Needless to say, organisations will need to be careful to ensure that any processing without consent (or falling under one of the other stipulated conditions) is clearly permissible as part of the public interest. In almost all cases, it will be simpler and safer to secure consent.

In addition to these requirements, personal data can only be processed for limited purposes, to a minimal extent and accurately. This ties into the requirement for transparency: the data subject must be aware of the nature of the processing, which will inform the 'limited purposes' and 'minimal extent'.

---

[30] EU GDPR, Article 6 (1) (e).
[31] EU GDPR, Article 6 (3).

Processing special categories of data (e.g. ethnicity, sexual orientation, health, etc.) is explicitly forbidden except in very specific circumstances.[32]

Retention of data

As noted earlier, data subjects have the right to be forgotten, at which point the data controller must erase all information held on them. In addition to this, however, personal data can also only be retained for limited periods, which should be clear to the data subject at the point at which they consent. This isn't a hard and fast rule, of course, as some personal data could be held effectively indefinitely (by public bodies for specific governmental purposes, for instance) and other processing, by its nature, may be ongoing.

Regardless of how long you intend to retain personal data, confidentiality and integrity must be secured – including against accidental loss, destruction or damage. This is particularly important and should be an extremely high priority for every organisation, not least because of the compulsory data breach reporting (which is explained later). While it's true that this is already a general requirement in almost all data protection regimes, you need to be sure that your information security practices cover the whole range of personal data – which, it's worth remembering, is now much broader – and that your suppliers and partners also understand and implement this.

---

[32] EU GDPR, Article 9.

The "one-stop shop"

The Regulation is intended to be a single scheme, applied consistently across the EU in order to maintain a common market and support the free flow of information.

The EU Data Protection Board created by the GDPR has several duties, including ensuring that any measures developed and adopted in member countries are consistent with the objectives of the GDPR. The Board will be composed of members of each state's lead supervisory authority (such as the Information Commissioner's Office in the UK), which should ensure that laws remain relatively consistent and with minimal impact on commerce.

Each state will determine a number of supervisory authorities or data protection authorities, who will be the local point of contact for all GDPR issues. This is the "one-stop shop" mechanism, which is intended to reduce the bureaucratic load involved in dealing with potentially complex pan-EU issues of data protection, anonymity and so on. Each state will also determine a lead supervisory authority or data protection authority, which will appoint a member to the EU Data Protection Board described above. It's quite likely that many countries will not bother with multiple supervisory authorities, simply because it is already centralised and there is little value in expanding the bureaucracy, but some non-unitary states may choose to operate these authorities on a regional basis, with a lead supervisory authority established at the national level.

Organisations processing personal data across a number of EU member states will deal with the data protection authority in their primary jurisdiction. This will cover all cross-border intra-EU data processing.

Records of data processing activities

Article 30 requires every data controller to retain a record of its data processing activities. This record needs to contain a specific set of information such that it is clear what data is being processed, where it is processed, how it is processed and why it is processed.

Equally, data processors are required under the same Article to keep a record of all processing carried out on behalf of a data controller. It should be noted that the definition of 'processing' is so wide that even organisations that solely collect, erase or destroy personal data are considered to be processing it.

These records need to be made available to the supervisory authority on request. There does not appear to be a requirement for a data controller to pay a fee to formally register with a supervisory authority.

Data protection impact assessments

What the GDPR calls data protection impact assessments (DPIAs) are now mandatory for technologies and processes that are likely to result in a high risk to the rights of data subjects. Much like other impact assessments, you'll need to ensure that you take advice from an appropriate authority.

The supervisory authority in each EU Member State may list the specific situations for which a DPIA is or is not required. Regardless of whether this is the case, most organisations should ensure that a DPIA is part of their risk assessment process regarding personal data, and is in line with their data protection by design and by default strategies.

There is a minor light on the horizon in this regard, though, in that a single DPIA can address a set of similar processing operations with comparable risks. This means that data controllers that run large numbers of processes on data sets can get a great deal of this burden out of the way relatively quickly.

Once again, the data controller is responsible for ensuring that DPIAs are conducted. It's not a requirement that the data controller actually performs the DPIA themselves, however, and in many cases where processing has been contracted to a third party, it may be more sensible to have it conducted by the data processor.

Data protection by design and by default

DPIAs neatly dovetail into considering data protection in the design phase of an application or process.

The notion of building privacy or data protection measures into applications and processes is not new. Nor is it new to consider privacy or data protection in the initial design phase, often called 'privacy by design'. The Regulation, however, makes this mandatory in Article 25. You should note that this includes processes, not just applications – if any of your processes could result in a loss of data protection, and you have not addressed this "by design and by default", you are likely to be held liable in the event of a data breach.

It is important to remember that the Regulation does not specify how much security you should apply, nor the specific measures you have to use – it's just a requirement for you to "implement appropriate technical and organisational measures".[33] The critical element of this will be ensuring that you can prove to the supervisory authority that you did indeed take data protection into account from the beginning of your design.

The Article does provide a caveat in that you can take the current state of the art into account (among other things), and it's possible that the only truly effective measure hasn't been invented yet, but it's unlikely to convince the supervisory authority. Instead, you'll probably be told that you should have determined that the risks were too great and that you shouldn't

---

[33] EU GDPR, Article 24 (1).

have gone ahead. That is, after all, part of considering the state of the art, and a significant part of data protection *by default*.

Controller/processor contracts

Where a controller contracts with a processor to process personal data, that processor must be able to provide "sufficient guarantees to implement appropriate technical and organisational measures"[34] that processing will comply with the GDPR and ensure data subjects' rights are protected. This requirement flows down the supply chain, so a processor cannot engage a second processor without the controller's explicit authorisation, which, of course, will also mean that the second processor has to supply the same guarantees.

This is simple good practice to start with, so it should not present any significant difficulty to organisations that already have robust information security practices in place for supplier contracts.

Regardless of your organisation's current state of information security, you should ensure that contractual arrangements are reviewed and updated. Ensure that responsibilities and liabilities between the controller and processor are stipulated. You will need to document data responsibilities very clearly to ensure there is no confusion, and you may have to accept that the increased risk levels and requirements for data protection measures may impact service costs.

Certifications to international standards, such as ISO/IEC 27001 are recognised as effective ways to demonstrate that appropriate technical and organisational measures have been implemented.

---

[34] EU GDPR, Article 28 (1).

The data protection officer

Many organisations will be required to appoint a data protection officer (DPO). Whether or not you need one is based on three conditions:

1. If the data is processed by a public authority or body, except for courts acting in their judicial capacity.

2. If the controller's or processor's core activities consist of processing operations that require regular and systematic monitoring of data subjects on a large scale.

3. If the controller's or processor's activities consist of processing large quantities of special categories of data and personal data relating to criminal convictions and offences.

In practice, these conditions will cover a large number of organisations, and it wouldn't be unusual to see companies appoint a DPO even if they're not strictly required to – it's quite possible that an organisation's ordinary business will one day spike or adjust slightly, which will suddenly require a DPO and, in any case, the range of requirements imposed by the GDPR on any organisation makes the appointment of an appropriately qualified person to this role a sensible risk-containment step.

The 'special categories of data' noted above are explained in Article 9 of the Regulation, which states that "personal data revealing racial or ethnic origin, political opinions, religious or philosophical beliefs, or trade-union membership, and the processing of genetic data, biometric data for the purpose of uniquely identifying a natural person, data concerning health or data concerning a natural person's sex life or sexual orientation shall be prohibited", although several caveats apply in order to permit valid uses of that information.

The DPO is appointed by the data controller and, where relevant, by the data processor, and a group of controllers and processors can share a single DPO as long as they are "easily accessible from each establishment". This means that organisations that may not have the resources to appoint a DPO for their own purposes can work with other such organisations to ensure they comply with the GDPR. Article 9 (6) makes it clear that the DPO can be employed under a service contract, so it's quite reasonable to expect that a number of suppliers will be willing to provide these services.

DPOs must be qualified for the role on the basis of expert knowledge of data protection law and practices, and being able to meet the requirements of Article 39 – "Tasks of the data protection officer". The role must report directly to top management, which should help ensure that data protection remains a key concern for the Board and senior managers, and also help to ensure that they remain well informed.

The DPO's duties generally revolve around ensuring that the data controller and data processor comply with all relevant data protection legislation, especially the GDPR. They should also offer advice, monitor data protection impact assessments and operate as the immediate contact for the supervisory authority. The DPO's name and contact details must also be included in a number of reports and also be published by the data controller or data processor; website privacy policies would be a sensible location for this.

Accountability and the Board

Given the magnitude of potential fines, the rights of data subjects to bring cases and claim compensation, and the prevalence and effectiveness of cyber crime, a GDPR breach should go straight onto the Board's risk register, and should remain high on Board and top management agendas.

It is also important to remember that, in most instances, the data controller will be accountable for failures of any data processor. That is not to say that the data processor gets off scot-free – they will also be held accountable – but it is critical that the Board and top management ensure that any third-party data processors they engage are operating in accordance with the Regulation, regardless of the jurisdiction in which they operate.

In addition to a DPO, there will be a number of other roles that will need a level of familiarity with the requirements of the GDPR – most HR staff, as well as middle and senior management in virtually any function that deals with personal data processed, stored or transmitted by the organisation. Staff awareness training should support the more focused training that is applied to managers.

Data breaches

In addition to being damaging for business, even if the authorities don't get involved, data breaches are much more strictly regulated under the GDPR. Under the current range of data protection regimes in the EU, many data breaches likely happen without the relevant authorities being notified, let alone the people who have been affected. The Regulation, however, mandates informing both the supervisory authority and the data subjects themselves.

There are, of course, some exemptions to the rules on notification, but it will be an essential part of best practice to ensure that you have processes in place to make these notifications in the event of a data breach. At the very least, your procedure for responding to a breach should include consulting with the DPO to confirm whether notification is necessary.

Data breach reports must be made within 72 hours of the data controller becoming aware of the breach. If that requirement is not met, the eventual report must be accompanied by an explanation for the delay. The notification must follow a specific format, which includes a requirement to describe the measures being taken to address the breach and mitigate its possible side effects. Where the breach may result in a high risk to the rights and freedoms of data subjects, they must be contacted "without undue delay". This contact will not be necessary if appropriate protective measures – essentially encryption – are in place to eliminate danger to data subjects.

Incident response and breach reporting processes could (and should) be expanded to cover all potential cyber breaches. Continual testing and maintenance of these processes will be important to ensure that you can meet the 72-hour deadline – and to demonstrate that you have taken action to protect data subjects' rights. Typically, incident response processes are covered in ISO27001 management systems.

Encryption

It would also be sensible to review existing arrangements around database and endpoint encryption. Organisations should already be encrypting mobile devices but, given the extent to which encryption could mitigate the impacts of a data breach, consideration should be given to extending encryption to cover all of the data collection, processing and storage processes.

Given the requirements around information security and continuity, DPOs need to be more than legal experts – they need a mix of qualifications that enable them to deal effectively with the legal requirements, as well as the operational requirement to demonstrate appropriate organisational and administrative measures.

When considering encryption standards, you would do well to follow best practice and seek out only FIPS 140-compliant solutions. FIPS 140 is the Federal Information Processing Standard established by the US and Canadian governments that sets out requirements for cryptography (it is not an encryption method in itself); in fact, in many cases it is a legal requirement that all cryptography modules must be FIPS 140-compliant. With that in mind, ensuring that your solutions meet this standard will not only protect personal data in line with the Regulation's requirements, it may also allow you access to new markets or clients.

It is also worth considering that encryption should not just be applied to storage of personal data, but may also be valuable (or necessary) for establishing secure connections when personal data will be transmitted. Encryption specialists will no doubt be aware that Secure Sockets Layer (SSL) encryption is no longer considered secure, and that Transport Layer Security (TLS) 1.2 or higher is really the new minimum for these connections.

International transfers

The GDPR deals specifically with situations where a controller or processor intends to transfer personal data outside the EU. Such international transfers are only legal if they comply with the conditions laid down in Chapter V of the GDPR, which are designed to ensure that the protections afforded to EU residents are not undermined by the transfer. These conditions require specific safeguards to be in place, and on the condition that data subject rights and effective legal remedies are available. This is comparable to the function of the previous requirements in the DPD, which meant that such information could be transferred to other countries as long as those countries had comparable data protection laws and measures in place.

As noted earlier, the former US-EU Safe Harbor Framework was dismantled in 2015. Under that framework, organisations in the US could attest that they adhered to seven principles and 15 frequently asked questions to meet the requirements of the DPD, which would then qualify them for certification under the framework and trouble-free access to the European market as a data processor. With this framework gone, there is a something of a vacuum.

Just prior to the GDPR being approved by the EU's governing bodies, a new agreement was signed between the EU and US: the EU-US Privacy Shield. While it has not yet come into effect, any personal data exchanged under the auspices of this agreement will be governed by the GDPR.

As an additional measure comparable to the Privacy Shield, the EU Commission may recognise some countries or international organisations as providing adequate protection for personal data. A list of these countries and organisations will be published and maintained, including noting where recognition has been removed. Data controllers and processors will be able to transfer personal data to those countries and organisations without any further authorisation or safeguards beyond those normally required under the GDPR.

Binding corporate rules

Outside of transfers to authorised entities or countries, international transfers can only take place if the controller or processor has put in place legally binding and enforceable arrangements to protect the rights of EU data subjects. Model binding corporate rules approved by the supervisory authority may be one such means. These model binding corporate rules have not yet been developed, but it would be reasonable to expect some statement on the topic prior to the GDPR's enforcement in 2018. It would be reasonable to expect that those rules will not be substantially different from rules already in place,[35] although they will need to account for the newer data subjects' rights, including the right to be forgotten.

In the meantime, you do not have to wait for model binding corporate rules in order to comply; you don't even have to use those when they do become available. Any organisation can develop its own binding corporate rules to secure personal data when transferring it to another country. The Regulation is very clear, however, as to what these rules must cover, so you will

---

[35] The UK's ICO has guidelines on binding corporate rules that are valid under the current regime. As it's likely these will be broadly comparable, this could prove a useful resource. *https://ico.org.uk/for-organisations/guide-to-data-protection/binding-corporate-rules/*.

need to consult Article 47 of the Regulation, and any rules you develop will need to be approved by the supervisory authority.

The GDPR states that codes of conduct and certifications to international standards are means by which controllers and processors may be able to identify organisations that will provide appropriate safeguards. In fact, the Regulation encourages supervisory authorities to draw up codes of conduct and to encourage the use of data protection certifications.[36]

As the controller and processor are accountable for the personal data they are processing, any agreement to transfer that data to a third party, outside the arrangements identified in the GDPR, will be illegal. This is particularly important when considering Cloud providers.

It should be noted that breaches of the Articles covering international transfers are subject to the highest administrative penalty.

Additional considerations

In addition to the GDPR, a number of other changes are impending or currently going through other legal processes. While they are not as comprehensive or backed by as much force, complying with requirements as they arise will be part of any sensible approach to compliance.

Changes to the 'Cookies Law'

The 'Cookies Law' – properly called the Directive on Privacy and Electronic Communications or the E-Privacy Directive – was controversial when it came into force in 2011 and it has

---

[36] EU GDPR, Article 57 (1).

remained so. While some authorities have since relaxed their initial declarations on enforcing the requirements (generally moving away from threats of action to simply providing advice and occasionally contacting organisations that make absolutely no effort[37]), there are still a host of websites decrying the Directive as ineffective, annoying and ridiculous.

The GDPR itself mentions cookies only once (in Recital 30), but does so to clarify that a cookie could be interpreted as an online identifier, which means that it falls under personal data and, therefore, the data subject must consent. This clearly asserts that all of the cookie notifications will need to follow the normal rules for consent, and forcing the supervisory authorities to act when non-compliance is discovered. This will not please the people who campaigned against the original Cookies Law (and who continue to do so).

The European Commission, meanwhile, announced in its 2016 work programme that it would be evaluating the E-Privacy Directive. This is likely to involve a few adjustments, in particular defining the exemptions for consent: currently, under both the E-Privacy Directive and the GDPR, consent is not necessary in certain conditions. Under the Regulation, for instance, processing of personal data is lawful if:

> processing is necessary for the performance of a contract to which the data subject is party or in order to take steps at the request of the data subject prior to entering into a contract;[38]

---

[37] The UK's ICO, for instance, now simply contacts organisations that people complain about, typically because the cookies in use are gathering too much data or are in breach of other data protection laws. As of May 2016, the ICO notes that it has written to 371 organisations since October 2012, and there is no indication that any further legal action has been taken. *https://ico.org.uk/action-weve-taken/cookies/*.
[38] EU GDPR, Article 6 (1) (b).

This exemption allows e-commerce businesses to, for instance, apply a cookie to track someone's purchases before they elect to actually buy them – the processing is a necessary step in the lead-up to a contract that the data subject will be entering (and providing consent for at that stage).

So, while it's possible that cookies will need to be more rigorously announced and consented to, it is equally possible that specific uses will be unaffected.

IP addresses

In the same breath that the Regulation declares cookies to be personal data, it also declares IP addresses to be the same. For privacy campaigners, this is bothersome. On the one hand, the Regulation does attempt to protect this information where it could be used to identify someone, but at the same time it appears to assert that an IP address could be interpreted to indicate a specific geographical location. In past court cases, it's been recognised that this is a misinterpretation of the way that IP addresses work, and several cases that have hinged on identifying individuals through their IP addresses have been thrown out on the grounds that an IP address cannot prove either who was using the device at the time, or, in many cases, precisely where they are.

At the time of writing, a case is being argued in Germany that, on the grounds of privacy, website and application providers should not store dynamic IP addresses for longer than necessary to deliver content. Germany's Advocate General also argues that IP addresses be considered personal data and that they should therefore not be used for anything other than basic content delivery. While this is still going through the court system, and will likely be reviewed again some time before the Regulation comes into force, it does tend to indicate that organisations that use IP addresses to do anything other than deliver content will need to find new methods to do so, or ensure that consent is sought and gained.

It would also be quite reasonable to expect that other aspects of personal data will end up being argued in courts across the EU, and that the full scope of 'personal data' will evolve over time as a result.

The EU Network and Information Security (NIS) Directive

The Network and Information Security (NIS) Directive is currently going through negotiations at various levels within the European Union. While the NIS is a directive and thus lacks the full legal weight of the GDPR, it aims to establish national-level cyber security functionalities that will have an impact on ordinary businesses and other organisations.

Where the GDPR seeks to protect personal data and the rights of the data subject, the NIS seeks to establish a "competent authority" for cyber security in each Member State. These authorities will be responsible for ensuring that national infrastructure is secure from cyber security threats and that the common citizen can have a degree of faith in the technologies they use daily. On top of this, a more secure national infrastructure is envisaged as having a positive economic impact because the stability and reliability of services will make it simpler to compete in the single digital marketplace.

For the ordinary organisation, it seems like the NIS will have little direct impact on them. This is not the case, however, as it will establish yet another authority to whom threats and incidents will need to be reported. Because it's likely that the "competent authority" will end up being a branch of the security services, it could also result in a degree of censorship regarding details of data breaches, which could, in turn, be in breach of the Regulation. This is a consideration that each Member State will determine in due course, but it's not likely to be without hiccups.

CHAPTER 4: COMPLYING WITH THE REGULATION

There are clearly a number of key points to observe in your approach to complying with the GDPR. Plenty of them will be resolved fairly simply and quickly, if only at the prompting of a third party or a data protection officer. Some, however, will require a great deal of work or specific expertise. This section of the book will discuss those things that are critical to observe and offer advice for staying on the right side of the law.

It's extremely important to remember that you must be compliant by the time the Regulation comes into force in May 2018. There is currently some time before this date, but it's sensible to determine what you need to do as soon as possible so that you can make appropriate plans and ensure that everything is ready in time. It would be a real shame to be among the first organisations hit with an administrative penalty under the Regulation.

Repercussions

It's been mentioned several times already, but it's worth reiterating that the heaviest fines that can be levied are considerable. For certain breaches of the Regulation, you could be fined up to €20 million or four percent of global annual turnover, whichever is greater. Note that the four percent is on turnover, not profit, and applies to the organisation's global turnover, so for large organisations this could be considerably more than €20 million, and for a number of companies could be close to or exceed a billion Euros.

It should also be noted that some organisations that are not involved in data processing can also face legal repercussions. Certification bodies involved in certification schemes in accordance with the Regulation, for instance, can face fines if they are found to be shirking their responsibilities. As such, it's possible for a single data breach to affect a large number of organisations – the data controller, any number of data processors involved in the data breach, and the certification body that approved the data processing.

Because these administrative penalties can be applied so broadly, it is very important to understand what your own obligations and exposure are. You should be certain to consult a legal expert if you are concerned that you might not be in compliance with the law.

It is also important to remember that these penalties are in addition to any other fines or legal costs that you may incur following a data breach. While fines from other regulators are unlikely to match the costs meted out under the GDPR, the compounding effects of other punitive measures could be significant. For instance, failure to meet the requirements of the PCI DSS could result in losing the ability to take card payments, civil disputes in court could result in additional fines, and reputational damage could strip you of your customers, clients and suppliers.

Ensuring that your organisation supports compliance with the Regulation from the very top will be critical to meeting your obligations – it would be difficult to implement all of the necessary measures without that level of support. As such, anyone responsible for implementing compliance will need to start by making this clear to their organisation's top management and ensuring that it is understood. Reiterating the severity of the punitive measures is likely to get their attention.

Understanding your data: where it is and how it is used

The GDPR deals with existing personal data as well as with how that data is to be processed, transmitted and stored in future. The first step toward compliance for most organisations will therefore be a data audit, identifying the personal data they already hold, who it has been shared with and where it is now held, and to determine what must be done with that data in order to comply with the GDPR.

This data audit process will necessarily include reviewing existing processes for gathering personal data, ensuring there are clearly identified business and legal grounds for that collection, and ensuring that all related processes will comply with the new regulation. Depending on the nature of your business, this could prove to be quite a broad exercise, showing points of egress and ingress where personal data goes out to a processor and then the processed result returns (assuming that the results of processing include personal data). You will also need to be quite clear about the information assets that actually constitute personal data – photographs, for instance, can be used to identify an individual and so will almost always be regarded as personal data.

You should also consider where the data resides physically. If you use a Cloud solution, for instance, you will need to know where the Cloud supplier is based and, if they're not based in the EU, whether they are able to provide sufficient assurances that they meet the Regulation's requirements (including, crucially, legal protections for data subjects and the presence of effective legal remedies). Equally, you should be sure to note any physical records of personal data that you might keep, including HR records, historical records (assuming the subjects are still living) and so on.

It would be sensible to carry out a DPIA in relation to information that you have already collected, in addition to any DPIAs necessary for future processing. This should highlight any weaknesses in your current operations that should be resolved ahead of the Regulation coming into force in 2018.

Documentation

The Regulation requires quite a bit of documentation. In addition to the explicit and implicit requirements for specific records (especially including proof of consent from data subjects), you should also ensure that you have documented how you comply with the GDPR so that you have some evidence to support your claims if the supervisory authority has any cause to investigate. If you suffer a data breach, for instance, being able to demonstrate that you have consistently applied best practice, that you have an audit trail showing that you notified them and any affected data subjects within the required timeframes, and that you have taken all the appropriate steps to mitigate the impacts of the data breach, will minimise the chance that you will be hit with a crippling fine.

There are different documentation requirements for data controllers and data processors, but the onus for the documentation being correct will generally be on the controller, because they're likely to suffer the consequences regardless of who is at fault. If you are a controller with a number of processing functions outsourced, it's worth gaining assurances that these functions are appropriately documented.

The following documentation is especially important, although, as noted above, it varies between data controllers and processors:

- Statements of the information you collect and process, and the purpose for processing[39]
- Records of consent from data subjects or their holder of parental responsibility[40]
- Records of processing activities under your responsibility[41]

---

[39] Full requirements in EU GDPR, Article 13.
[40] Full requirements in EU GDPR, Articles 7 and 8.
[41] Full requirements in EU GDPR, Article 30.

- Documented processes for protecting personal data – an information security policy, cryptography policy and procedures, etc.

Appropriate technical and organisational measures, and ISO/IEC 27001

Article 24 says that data controllers must implement "appropriate technical and organisational measures to ensure and to be able to demonstrate that the processing is performed in accordance with the Regulation". This Article makes it clear that these measures must include implementing appropriate data protection policies. Critically, it also states that controllers can use adherence to approved codes of conduct or management system certifications "as an element by which to demonstrate compliance with [their] obligations".[42]

While it's likely that supervisory authorities will develop their own schemes and trust seals, and that they'll recognise certain standards as meeting the GDPR's core requirements (as discussed later), achieving certification to a widely recognised information security standard will not only help to meet the requirements, it will also provide a good basis for attaining any necessary certifications or requirements that may arise in the future.

An ISO/IEC 27001 information security management system (ISMS) should be the starting point for organisations seeking to ensure they can demonstrate "appropriate technical and organisational measures" with respect to their GDPR obligations. The ISO27001 risk-based approach to selecting information security controls is reflected in the GDPR requirement that controllers and processors should, on the basis

---

[42] EU GDPR, Article 24 (3).

of and proportionate to identified risk, implement appropriate technical and organisational controls to:

- ensure the ongoing confidentiality, integrity, availability and resilience of processing systems and services;
- ensure the security of the personal data; and
- ensure the ability to restore availability following an incident.

They should also have a process for regular testing, assessing and reviewing the effectiveness of the selected measures. As ISO/IEC 27001 is the only independent, internationally recognised data security standard that also has a widely accepted certification scheme, it seems logical that ISO27001 – with in-built and appropriate business continuity arrangements – should be fundamental to organisational GDPR compliance strategies.

The fact that ISO27001 is also the default management system for protecting organisations against cyber crime doubles its benefit. While cyber crime is not directly addressed in the Regulation, it is an increasingly common cause of data breaches, and regularly associated with the largest and most damaging breaches.

Implementing an ISO27001 ISMS involves building a holistic framework of processes, people and technologies in order to secure information. It should address the organisation's internal and external contexts – such as the requirements of the GDPR – and the needs of interested parties – which would naturally include data subjects. Once it's been established, the ISMS should systematically reduce information security risks on an ongoing and evolving basis through a process of self-examination and remediation. Crucially, the measures that you implement to secure information are taken on the basis of a thorough risk assessment that identifies threats and vulnerabilities affecting the organisation's information assets (which will certainly include any personal data or processing of personal data).

While an ISMS can take some time to develop and mature, it is an excellent first step in demonstrating that you take data protection seriously, and the costs of implementation can often be offset by the efficiency improvements and improved market position.

Any appropriate trust marks should be integrated into the ISMS as they become available.

Standards, schemes and trust seals

Compliance with the international information security standard ISO/IEC 27001 will help organisations demonstrate that they have endeavoured to comply with the GDPR requirements.

The Regulation suggests that approved certifications and schemes will appear, which may be developed locally (by supervisory authorities, for instance) or across the EU (by the Commission or EU Data Protection Board, for instance) to prove compliance with a set of practices that meet the requirements of the GDPR. One or more such schemes to provide GDPR-specific certification are likely to emerge, but it will be some time before there is clarity on this front.

It's also possible that some form of trust seal may be developed, much like the SOC 3 audit (but hopefully more affordable). In the meantime, organisations should certainly adapt an existing ISO27001 management system, or start working toward ISO27001 with a strong GDPR emphasis, perhaps with ISO/IEC 27018 (Code of Practice for protecting personal data in the Cloud) included in the scope. Some certification bodies are already conducting audits that include ISO/IEC 27018 in the management system scope.

Securing supplier relationships

The data audit described earlier will help you to identify which supplier relationships you have that need to account for the Regulation due to the movement of personal data between you.

The most obvious upshot of this will be reviewing your various contracts with third parties. You should ensure that your service-level agreements, and procurement and outsourcing processes, are reviewed in line with the requirements of the GDPR. This is especially important if you are the data controller in the relationship, as you will be equally liable for any breaches that occur as a result of a supplier's failure to preserve data protection. This should also include restrictions on the use of processors further down the supply chain in order to ensure the security of personal data at every point in the processing.

You will also need to check your suppliers of Cloud services, remote servers and so on. While these are remote services, they're often integrated into the organisation's business practices as if they are managed locally, so it can be easy to forget about them. As noted earlier, you should also ensure that these service providers are either within the EU, or that you are able to preserve the relationship through the Privacy Shield or binding corporate rules. If you cannot secure these assurances, or there is difficulty having the service provider approved under the Regulation, you'll need to work fast to secure a more local or trustworthy supplier.

In addition to ensuring that the organisations you work with are in compliance with the Regulation, you also need to ensure that any data transfers are secure. This is a more practical consideration (use of encryption, etc.), but it should also be agreed with the supplier and included in contracts and service-level agreements.

CHAPTER 5: INDEX OF THE REGULATION

Chapter I – General provisions

1. Subject-matter and objectives
2. Material scope
3. Territorial scope
4. Definitions

Chapter II – Principles

5. Principles relating to processing of personal data
6. Lawfulness of processing
7. Conditions for consent
8. Conditions applicable to child's consent in relation to information society services
9. Processing of special categories of personal data
10. Processing of personal data relating to criminal convictions and offences
11. Processing which does not require identification

Chapter III – Rights of the data subject

Section 1 – Transparency and modalities

12. Transparent information, communication and modalities for the exercise of the rights of the data subject

Section 2 – Information and access to personal data

13. Information to be provided where personal data are collected from the data subject
14. Information to be provided where personal data have not been obtained from the data subject
15. Right of access by the data subject

CHAPTER 6: EU GDPR RESOURCES

IT Governance has a number of resources to make compliance with the GDPR painless or, at the very least, much simpler. These range from books like the one you're reading (but generally more detailed), documentation toolkits and training courses, through to data audits and a variety of consultancy options.

Certified EU GDPR Foundation training course

This comprehensive training course will offer a solid introduction to the GDPR, and provide a practical understanding of the implications and legal requirements of the regulation, culminating in an official certification from the International Board of IT Governance Qualifications (IBITGQ).

www.itgovernance.co.uk/shop/p-1795-eu-general-data-protection-training.aspx

Certified EU GDPR Practitioner training course

This course will enable delegates to fulfil the role of data protection officer (DPO) under the GDPR, and will cover the Regulation in depth, including implementation requirements, the necessary policies and processes, and important elements of effective data security management.

www.itgovernance.co.uk/shop/p-1824-certified-eu-general-data-protection-regulation-practitioner-training-course.aspx

EU GDPR Documentation toolkit

A full set of policies and procedures enabling your organisation to comply with the EU GDPR, these templates are fully customisable and significantly reduce the burden of developing the necessary documents to achieve legal compliance.

www.itgovernance.co.uk/shop/p-1796-eu-general-data-protection-regulation-documentation-toolkit.aspx

Privacy impact assessments training

This one-day course is designed to provide delegates with the practical knowledge needed to perform a privacy impact assessment (PIA) and help their organisations identify the most effective way to fulfil their data protection obligations.

PIA Workshop

www.itgovernance.co.uk/shop/p-1640-privacy-impact-assessment-pia-workshop.aspx

EU General Data Protection Regulation (GDPR) – An Implementation and Compliance Guide

This comprehensive manual provides detailed insights into the EU GDPR and offers practical implementation advice on setting up and managing a privacy programme.

www.itgovernance.co.uk/shop/p-1829-eu-general-data-protection-regulation-gdpr-an-implementation-and-compliance-guide.aspx

EU GDPR data flow audit

Organisations should have a clear idea of
the personal data being held, where it
originated from, and who it can be shared
with. A data audit is a key part of a data
protection compliance regime.

www.itgovernance.co.uk/shop/p-1831-gdpr-data-flow-audit.aspx

EU GDPR Consultancy and Transition services

Organisations that need access to experienced consultancy
support – whether to help plan the implementation of a GDPR-
compliant management system, or to plan and execute a
transition from a current DPD regime to compliance with the
GDPR – can draw on the experienced consultancy support
from IT Governance, whose practitioners have substantial data
protection and privacy experience, and who are at the forefront
of designing processes that will meet the new GDPR
requirements.

www.itgovernance.co.uk/dpa-compliance-consultancy.aspx

ITG RESOURCES

IT Governance is a leading global provider of IT governance, risk management and compliance solutions, with a special focus on cyber resilience, data protection, PCI DSS, ISO 27001 and cyber security.

In an increasingly punitive and privacy-focused business environment, we are committed to helping businesses protect themselves and their customers from the perpetually evolving range of cyber threats. Our deep industry expertise and pragmatic approach help our clients improve their defences and make key strategic decisions that benefit the entire business. We are unique in our ability to provide everything you need, including standards, tools, books, training, and consultancy and support as detailed in Chapter 6.

Publishing Services

IT Governance Publishing (ITGP) is the world's leading IT-GRC publishing imprint that is wholly owned by IT Governance Ltd.

With books and tools covering all IT governance, risk and compliance frameworks, we are the publisher of choice for authors and distributors alike, producing unique and practical publications of the highest quality, in the latest formats available, which readers will find invaluable.

www.itgovernancepublishing.co.uk is the website dedicated to ITGP. Other titles published by ITGP that may be of interest include:

- An Introduction to Information Security and ISO27001

  www.itgovernance.co.uk/shop/p-357.aspx

- Information Security A Practical Guide

  www.itgovernance.co.uk/shop/p-1701.aspx

- Nine Steps to Success: An ISO 27001:2013 Implementation Overview, Third edition

  www.itgovernance.co.uk/shop/p-963.aspx

We also offer a range of off-the-shelf toolkits that give comprehensive, customisable documents to help users create the specific documentation they need to properly implement a management system or standard. Written by experienced practitioners and based on the latest best practice, ITGP toolkits can save months of work for organisations working towards compliance with a given standard.

Please visit www.itgovernance.co.uk/shop/c-129-toolkits.aspx to see our full range of toolkits.

Books and tools published by IT Governance Publishing (ITGP) are available from all business booksellers and the following websites:

www.itgovernance.eu   *www.itgovernanceusa.com*

www.itgovernance.in   *www.itgovernancesa.co.za*

www.itgovernance.asia.

Newsletter

You can stay up to date with the latest developments across the whole spectrum of IT governance subject matter, including risk management, information security, ITIL and IT service management, project governance, compliance and so much more, by subscribing to our newsletter.

Simply visit our subscription centre and select your preferences:

www.itgovernance.co.uk/newsletter.aspx.